T0128543

AlaynaStrong

*An unexpected journey
through Aplastic Anemia*

Ashley Numbers

Proofreading and Editing by Skylar Blumenauer

authorHOUSE®

AuthorHouse™
1663 Liberty Drive
Bloomington, IN 47403
www.authorhouse.com
Phone: 1 (800) 839-8640

Published by AuthorHouse 05/22/2020

ISBN: 978-1-7283-6211-3 (sc)
ISBN: 978-1-7283-6210-6 (hc)
ISBN: 978-1-7283-6209-0 (e)

Library of Congress Control Number: 2020909143

Print information available on the last page.

I want to dedicate this book to my daughter, Alayna. You are the one who made me a mommy for the first time, the one who taught me what love is truly all about. You are so brave and courageous, I know you will do great things in your life, you already have been through more in your young life than most. I love you to the moon and back, to the stars and back, to infinity, and beyond.

"Though she be but little, she is fierce!"

-William Shakespeare

Contents

Chapter 1

I Do

* July 19, 2019 *

Bliss. Pure bliss filled my heart as I looked out upon my gathered family. Tomorrow, I would marry my fiancé. Tonight, however, I sit with my family to celebrate spending the rest of our lives together. We had chosen a nearby Amish restaurant for dinner. It was a wonderful evening filled with love and laughter. It was so heartwarming to see everyone together in one place, as most of Chris' family lives out of state. But looking back, nothing could have prepared me for the storm ahead.

Chris and I met through mutual friends when I was eighteen, and he was twenty-six. Even though we weren't married yet, we already have two beautiful children. Our daughter Alayna was a feisty, big-hearted three-year-old; our son Michael, or Mikey as we call him, was a loving, laidback and playful one-year-old. Nerves of the next day began kicking in, despite spending the last nine years of our life together.

After dinner, Chris and I decided to take the kids for a swim. We headed back to his dad's hotel in a nearby town. While changing Alayna, a bruise caught my attention. We'd been keeping a close eye on it after her last episode of bruises. The mark, now featuring an odd bump in the middle, had been there for a few days. Rewind to two weeks earlier, Alayna had horrible bruising on her legs that went away fairly quickly. Considering it was summer, she spent a lot of time outside at home and at daycare. I just assumed she was playing a little too rough since there weren't any reported falls.

Chris, his dad, and stepmom were also in the room, and everyone agreed with me that the bruise looked quite abnormal. The bump unsettled me more than I cared to admit. Alayna, however, seemed fine. The bruise didn't bother her at all, which reassured me slightly as she had no other symptoms. After talking to Chris, we agreed to call the doctor the following Monday. Alayna and Mikey had a blast swimming with their Papa Mike. Chris and I decided to get a drink while the kids swam and hang out with his mom and sister. After the kids had their fun, we took them home and got them ready for bed. Making sure they were settled, I took off for my hotel. I wanted to at least keep some traditions the night before my wedding.

My mom shared a room with me as I settled down for the last night before entering married life. While having a couple of drinks, we shared a pleasant conversation. Enjoying the rare quietness, I finished the final touches of the wedding, gathering money and paper checks for those who still needed paying. Nerves still ate away at me, as I fell asleep thinking of the coming day. My wedding day.

* July 20, 2019 *

It was here. My wedding day finally arrived, and I was beyond excited. Of course, very nervous too. My mom and I met my sister-in-law Bre and cousins at the Metropolitan Centre, our wedding venue, to begin setting up. The early morning was already muggy, and the day was slowly turning into the hottest of the summer, just our luck. After directing them to different tasks, I headed to get my hair and makeup done.

Before I knew it, the afternoon had come, and I was standing in the second-floor conference room of the Centre, getting ready to put on my dress. As I watched people come and go, frantically finishing last-minute responsibilities, my nerves were in full effect. Though it was a difficult task, I managed to gather my parents, my brother Nick, Bre, and a few close cousins to take a couple of shots. It was a fun experience, but it didn't help my nerves as much as I wanted.

A couple of minutes later, I was sitting alone on the couch. Then, in walked Alayna. She was wearing an adorable white dress with her light brown hair curled up into a bun. She looked so beautiful. As she ran to me, a sudden sensation of calmness overcame me. All she could talk about was how excited she was to throw her flower petals. Her energy was contagious, and she gave me the calm I needed for what was coming.

The ceremony was short and sweet, held on the rooftop patio of the Centre. Chris and I both hate being the center of attention, and that paired with the unbearable heat made a quick ceremony. One of Chris's best friends, who was also a good family friend, officiated the wedding. Alayna was our flower girl, and she made sure every part of that aisle was covered. Mikey was our ring bearer, though he had more fun playing with the flower petals on the ground.

Amongst being hot, the day was extremely windy on the rooftop. At one point, an umbrella almost flew away. Several had to leap to save it. During our vows, Mikey kept trying to hand his prized flower petals to Chris. That brought a couple of chuckles. Nevertheless, it was my type of perfect, with my closest family and friends surrounding us.

An hour later, the rest of our guests began arriving for the reception. The Centre's dining room was decorated beautifully in our teal and black color scheme. We ate, drank, and danced the night away. Within a few hours, Mikey was out, tired from the eventful day. He can fall asleep anywhere. Alayna, however, spent her night on the stage, dancing away for everyone with her friends. They especially loved performing their favorite song, "Baby Shark" for us.

Alayna ended up developing another bruise without cause. The large, dark discoloration appeared on the underside of her arm. Thankfully, it didn't cause her any pain or stop her from dancing the night away. Despite the wonderfulness of the day, the storm was still brewing.

Sunday morning, Chris and I woke up to get breakfast. Or rather, should I say *I* went down for some breakfast. Chris wasn't feeling the greatest after all of the activities and drinking that went on after the wedding. After eating, I returned to our room and began going through our gifts and cards. Once they were all opened, I began to pack everything up, excited to get back home to the kiddos. Chris's sister took them back home last night.

The kids were beyond excited to see us. It was nice visiting with family who was staying with us, talking about the wedding and looking through pictures. I was officially Mrs. Numbers! What could go wrong? The father of my amazing children was finally my husband, and I couldn't have been happier. The wedding had gone smoothly, and we couldn't help but feel like we were on cloud nine.

* The Next Morning *

When Alayna woke up and ate breakfast the next morning, I was in shock when I saw her legs. It looked as if someone had thrown her down a flight of stairs two times over again. Which, of course, didn't happen. Theories began flying through my head. She hadn't fallen or got hit. She did dance the night away two nights ago at the wedding. But the terrible bruises were too dark for that to be the cause.

As we originally planned, I called her doctor's office at 8 am. I had forgotten her primary doctor, Dr. Kantaras, did not come in on Mondays but would return Tuesday. I was hesitant about waiting that long, but I made a difficult choice and decided to do so. Alayna's doctor knows her and our family best, having been with her since she was born.

About a month earlier, Alayna had a weird rash on her forearm. It looked to be petechiae, tiny, round spots that develop from bleeding beneath the skin. Chris had taken her to the doctor that day since I couldn't get off of work. Dr. Kantaras wasn't in, so they saw a different one. He ended up brushing it off, saying Alayna had no other dire symptoms and seemed fine otherwise. Chris didn't demand bloodwork like I had asked him too, which upset me slightly.

We went on with our day. Chris's mom and sisters were leaving to go back to their New Jersey home later on. His other sister Michelle, her husband, and infant son were staying with us until Tuesday, after spending the entire previous week with us. We wanted to do something fun before they drove home and ended up going bowling. We had a fantastic time. It was the kids' first-time bowling, and it was adorable to watch them. Little did I know, this was the calm before the storm.

Chapter 2

Room 5625

* Tuesday, July 23, 2019 *

The day our lives changed. We took Alayna to her doctor appointment and I just had this gut feeling something was terribly wrong. Although she seemed healthy, her bruising was a lot worse and she had petechiae now on her face and all over her body. We sat in the waiting room until a nurse called Alayna's name. She brought us to a room to wait for her doctor to come in, which only took a few minutes. Dr. Kantaras walked into the room, took one look at Alayna, and had a look of concern on her face. After a rather fast examination, she ordered bloodwork, stat. Having been with this doctor all of Alayna's life, Chris and I knew she didn't get worked up over small, easy fixes. The concern written all over her face confirmed my gut feeling that something was not right. The only explanation she had for us was a possible blood clotting disorder. Her few words made my worry even worse. As we departed for stat care, she warned us to make sure Alayna didn't fall or hit her head in the meantime. Chris drove the kids and me to the nearest stat care, where we had to wait almost an hour to get the bloodwork. While waiting, I could feel the pressure of the eyes staring at Alayna. If I was honest, I couldn't blame them. With her bruises and red marks, she looked beaten. After what felt like an eternity, Alayna was finally called back. The phlebotomist, which is a doctor trained to draw blood, had Chris hold Alayna in his arms while I held Mikey. She screamed and cried, I could see the terror in her eyes. I felt terrible and helpless. But I had to be strong for her, my strong little girl who did amazing for her first time getting blood drawn. After, we stopped and got lunch to take home. At home, I waited for her doctor to call with the results. Not very patiently, however. My nerves were eating away at me as I waited for the lab results. Once 4 o'clock came, we still hadn't heard anything. I eventually caved in and called the doctors, leaving a message to get back soon. Within twenty minutes, her doctor called us back.

"I apologize, when you called I was on the phone with Akron Children's Hospital making arrangements," she greeted me. I went blank and couldn't process the words I wanted to because the tears started coming, that mom gut feeling knew this wasn't good. She then went on to say that Alayna's bloodwork was showing a dangerously low platelet count of 7,000. Normal range for platelets in a human body is 250,000-450,000. She added that she talked to the on-call doctor at the hospital and they are waiting for us and have a bed ready as she will need a platelet transfusion and need to be admitted for observation, again advised us to make sure Alayna did not hit her head. With such a low platelet level, a bump on the head could be deadly because the platelets are what help your blood clot. No platelets to help your blood clot means uncontrollable bleeding.

After I hung up, I was a mess. My only goal was to hold it together in front of the kids. Chris had watched the whole exchange, and I tried to explain what she had said, but it was hard. We have never had a scare like this happen before with either kid. I was in shock that something like this happened and my question is how now? What is going on in her body? Of course, in the middle of the chaos, Michelle and her husband were still with us, preparing to take off for the airport. They were heading back home to California today, and they were finishing their packing. Offering their condolences, Michelle and her husband felt just as worried and helpless as us. Chris went to pack an overnight bag for Alayna and the two of us while I picked up my phone. With my voice breaking and tears in my eyes, I called my brother Nick. I asked him and his wife, Bre, to stay the night with Mikey and our pets. Within half an hour, Nick and Bre had arrived at our house. We handed Mikey off to them and started our drive up to the hospital. Everyone knows in cases like this, the internet was the last place you wanted to turn to, but always the first place you ended up. As I scrolled through my phone, endless possibilities of nightmarish diseases popped out at me. Our poor little girl did nothing deserving of this.

Alayna's doctor had told me on the phone that once we arrived at the hospital we were told to go through ER to get admitted. After a short wait in the waiting room they got us back fairly quick and a nurse did Alayna's vitals. After they finished, a doctor walked in. She introduced herself, telling us she would escort us to the floor where they had a room prepared for Alayna. "Now," she said, looking at us very seriously. "The floor Alayna is going to be staying on is the oncology and hematology unit."

The two words emptied every thought in my head and left my ears ringing. I knew what the words meant. Hematology is the study and diagnosis of blood diseases, and oncology is cancer that falls beneath that category. I just broke down thinking to myself "Oh my god, my child could have cancer." It took all I had in me to not want to just fall to the ground and cry right there but I had to stay strong for Alayna. "Remember, this doesn't necessarily mean Alayna has cancer, but more testing still needs to be done so we can rule out possibilities," she went on to explain. Chris and I turned to each other, and I could see my fear reflected in his eyes. I knew the same thought was going through his head, oh my God, our child could have cancer. Off in the distance, I heard the doctor making arrangements for Alayna to ride to her room in a wagon. The wagon ride made her extremely excited, and that's when it hit me. I thought to myself that Alayna was just bowling yesterday and before that dancing the night away at our wedding, she will be fine. There weren't any for sure answers yet, so I couldn't let the possibilities consume me. We have this three-year-old child looking at us for reassurance at times when she's seeing all of these strangers who are about to poke and prod her. We have to treat her like a three-year-old and try our greatest to make the best of the situation at hand. Alayna enjoyed her ride while daddy pulled the wagon. We followed a volunteer down halls and rode an elevator up a couple of floors. Then, the doors opened. The sign on the wall caught my eye right away. It read, "The Showers Family Center for Childhood Cancer and Blood Disorders."

Alayna had no idea what was going to happen which was heart wrenching. But, I knew there would be more blood work involved and of course an IV. Heck, she was just enjoying a fun ride in a wagon. We arrived in front of a door with Alayna's name printed on a tag on the same sign that showed her room number. Room 5625. I noticed all of the patient rooms that we passed had vibrant colored walls for the kids. Alayna's room was orange. A nurse named Kelsey came in and helped us get settled. She was very friendly, talking to her helped ease my nerves slightly. As we were talking, the Physician Assistant, Terri, came in. Terri was just as kind as Kelsey and gave us a rundown of their plans for the night. Kelsey would draw labs to compare them with the ones taken earlier in the day. From there, it all depended on the results. Everyone was so fantastic with Alayna. Watching Alayna get an IV for the first time was terrible. Kelsey couldn't find a good enough vein that she felt comfortable with and didn't want to have to poke Alayna again if it didn't work. I appreciated her honesty. Another nurse came in, Kimmie, she was great. She was so reassuring and smiley. She was able to find a suitable vein and completed the IV. I quickly learned how traumatizing it was to hold your child down, tell them everything was going to be okay, and watch as needles poked into them. They were able to draw the blood they needed for labs and start fluids.

An hour comes and goes, and it is about 8 pm before I know it. Alayna was finally able to eat a little bit of dinner after the long day she had. A knock on the door sounded and in walked Terri, a doctor following right behind her. He introduced himself as Dr. Farris. Looking back and forth between their faces, I could tell we were about to have a conversation they didn't want to be having. I was sitting on the bed with Alayna and Chris was on a couch, we both looked at each other in fear when we saw someone else come in with Terri. He and Terri both sat down on the couch and explained Alayna's bloodwork and possible reasons that could cause low platelets and why this was happening. The labs were the same as earlier and they also mentioned her white cell count being a little low. The main cause of their concern was Leukemia. Leukemia is cancer affecting the bone marrow and blood-forming tissues. To determine if this was truly the cause, they would need to perform a bone marrow biopsy the next morning. After explaining all of us, they answered any questions we had very thoroughly and not rushed at all.

Talk about being high on cloud nine after the wedding, to three days later, come crashing down. Once they left, Chris and I sat in silence while Alayna watched the TV. We cried together, and we were there for each other. But we were both terrified. At that moment, I would have given and done anything to trade spots with her. After gathering ourselves together, we each called our parents to fill them in. I texted my cousin Heather, who promised to keep the rest of our family up to date.

Every call I made to each parent, the tears would start all over again. No matter how hard I tried, I couldn't keep it together. Alayna kept asking why Mommy was crying. I told her I didn't like to watch her get poked and I was sad it had to happen, for I had no other answer. I reassured her she was so strong and brave for the doctors. Once she believed me, I slipped away to the bathroom in her room to pull myself together.

That night, they ended up giving Alayna a bag of platelets, which she responded well too, without any reactions. I have never seen any type of blood transfusion happen before. The platelets were a clear color and they fall with gravity through the IV as they are not pumped in. Fifteen minutes after the transfusion started, they took vitals to make sure no reactions were happening. A platelet transfusion goes fairly quickly, considering they are pulled through the tube by gravity. It didn't last longer than twenty minutes. We did end up finding out Alayna's blood type is AB positive, which is rare. Those with AB+ blood types are considered universal receivers considering they can receive nearly any blood type.

That night was hard for me. My whole world had just flipped inside out. It was as if my worst nightmare come true. I struggled to fall asleep because my mind kept repeating the same questions over and over. Why my child? Why her? Why does this have to happen to her, and what did I do to deserve this? She is the happiest, silliest girl you can find. She doesn't deserve to go through this. No child does.

Chapter 3

Biopsy

I awoke the next day, and the previous day came flooding back to me. I remembered what today was. It was Biopsy Day. After getting up and moving, Dr. Farris greeted us with a good morning. He brought with him another doctor, which he introduced as Dr. Fargo. Dr. Fargo would be performing the biopsy on Alayna. They gave us a rundown on the schedule of the day, informing us what time everything was going to happen. I felt trapped in a bad dream, and I wasn't able to get out. Sick to my stomach, I wasn't able to eat breakfast. I had to put on a fake smile for my child, who woke up ready to play. Alayna didn't understand anything that was about to happen. I didn't know how to explain it all to her. This situation was hard, and it didn't help that it was all happening so fast. Crazy to think, a couple of days ago, my biggest worry was my wedding day going smooth.

Alayna seems completely normal, she's not "sick". With all that she was going through, you'd expect a sickly child. On the bright side, we did receive news that Alayna's platelets were up to 69,000. That was excellent news to hear. Although it's still very low, it was encouraging to hear. The nurse informed us that on this floor that is a great number for platelets. The hospital never gives out platelets to patients with counts higher than 10,000. She was at the median, where if she needed it badly enough, the number could drop so she could get more.

Ten o'clock came sooner than I hoped. A new lady knocked on our door before coming in and introducing herself as Brenda. She was the hospital's child life specialist. She got down on Alayna's level and explained to her what was happening as far as the biopsy. She was very good at explaining it to her in kid terms. After making sure Alayna understood, Brenda came back to talk to us. She just had a warm glow around her, I felt comfort talking with her. Brenda offered to let one of us stay in the procedure room with her, but we both declined. I already get nauseous around blood and needles, let alone it being from my child. It would've been too hard to watch.

Once we were down in the procedure room, a wave of faintness overcame me. The nerves, the information, and everything from the (not even) past twenty-four hours hit me at once. In general, out of Chris and me, I am the one who gets nervous with hospitals. Surprisingly, they let Chris and me in the room while they were prepping Alayna's sedation. Alayna had never gotten sedated before this, and the whole situation made me nervous.

Chris and I were both pretty choked up, and I think the doctors could tell. Alayna was already overwhelmed by the number of people in the room. To help calm her down, they gave her a medicine that was supposed to relax her. As they were prepping her, the anesthesiologist explained to us very thoroughly what they were doing and what to expect. As he began to give Alayna the sedation medicine he warned us that she might feel a slight burning sensation. As soon as the words left his mouth, Alayna began to cry, screaming that her arm was burning as they gave her the medicine through her current IV.

I will never forget her screams and the way she reached out to Chris during that moment asking for "Daddy." You could see how uncomfortable the sensation made her. She wrapped her little arms around his neck ever so tightly, and within seconds, fell limp in his arms. I guess being in the doctoral profession, it was just a typical day for a child to cry and yell before undergoing any procedure like this. But for a mother and father, witnessing their child go through that was terrible.

Chris laid Alayna gently back on the bed, and I lost it. We both did. I couldn't stand seeing my baby girl lay there, looking so lifeless. Brenda escorted us back to the waiting room. She reassured us we did amazing with Alayna. After she walked out, we held each other and cried. Within ten minutes, Brenda was coming back in to get us. Luckily, it was a quick procedure.

She took us back to the procedure room where Alayna and the doctor were waiting for us. They told us everything went well, and we just needed to wait for Alayna to wake up. After about twenty minutes or so, she began to wake up, very groggily. Thankfully, she didn't remember the pain of the sedation. Alayna got another wagon ride, to her delight. We laid her down in it and made our way back up to her room. Shortly after she was back up and playing, without any pain, like nothing had happened this past hour.

The doctors thought it would be best for us to spend another night, pending the biopsy results. Thankfully, nothing much happened for the rest of the day. Brenda was able to find a pink car to push Alayna around in, so of course, we had to go around the hallway multiple times. She also found some fairy wings and a magic wand. Alayna would wave her magic wand, and the lights of the playroom would turn off, making stars show up on the ceiling. She got a big kick out of that.

The next morning was the same routine. The doctors came in, and we talked everything over. Only a couple of the results were in from biopsy. They didn't anticipate the rest coming in for another week or so. At this point, from what they were seeing, it was showing a negative for Leukemia. While that was great news, it wasn't for sure. Alayna's bruising was looking much better as well.

Alayna had a pretty laid-back day. Her highlight, though, was meeting Kyle Kaiser! Kaiser is an Indy racing driver who was passing through on his way to a race. They got a couple of pictures together, and she enjoyed talking with him. After he left, we spent the rest of the day baking cookies. The volunteers brought in a toaster oven with dough, icing, and sprinkles. They made Alayna feel special and took excellent care of her.

Day 3 came, and Alayna's platelets were up to 79,000! They went up even more overnight, all by themselves. While there was still not an answer to what was causing this, the doctors were almost positive it wasn't cancer. I told myself, it was just some virus she caught that is causing this, she is on the upswing now. The doctors made a follow-up appointment in 2-3 weeks to go over all of the results from the bone marrow biopsy and check up on Alayna. We were free to go after the two nights spent in the hospital.

They advised us that Alayna should take it easy, as their biggest concern was making sure she didn't fall or hit her head. The easy bruising was from such a low platelet count, the blood was literally puddling under her skin. It was also best to keep her out of daycare since her white blood cell count was still low. With them being that low, she could easily catch a virus or infection from being around other kids. They also told us to call in sooner if anymore bruising or petechiae showed up. It was a relief the doctors were pretty positive that this wasn't cancer, but still frustrating that they haven't been able to find an answer yet.

After about five symptom-free days, Alayna started developing a petechial rash again. I called the hospital's clinic, where we originally scheduled her follow-up appointment. They were able to get Alayna in at the end of the week. In the meantime, Dr. Farris called us. More results came in from the biopsy and still showed no signs of cancer. I had plenty of time to think about possible causes in the past couple of days. I told him to add a tick bite on the list of possible causes since we did live in a wooded area with lots of trees.

Finally, the end of the week came, and so did Alayna's appointment. It was a funny thing, counting down the days until you could take your child back to the hospital. Usually, you dread those visits, but I wanted to find an answer. I was curious about what her blood work would look like after so many days without checking. The nurses took care of a finger poke, and Dr. Fargo did his exam on Alayna. The lab results came in, and of course, Alayna's platelets were a count of around 16,000. They advised us to make an added appointment in a couple of days for another platelet transfusion. I was astounded. I thought that she was finally on the upswing of things. What is going on with my sweet little girl?

We kept the original follow-up appointment, hoping to finally get a diagnosis by the end of the following week. A few days later, we took Alayna back in for her platelet transfusion. Just our luck, her platelets were under 10,000 like they suspected they would be, so Alayna was able to receive her transfusion. Watching the nurses have to give her yet another IV was heartbreaking. They, again, had trouble finding a vein.

I requested the PIC team to come up with their ultrasound machine. It's a team of health care professionals specially trained in vascular access. They use an ultrasound machine to help guide them and find a decent vein. The team was incredible with Alayna. From there on out I requested they do Alayna's IV when needed. Before leaving for home, they gave us a standing order to take to our local hospital. The order was so they could start checking Alayna's blood counts at the beginning of the week. With the order, we wouldn't have to drive the hour-long trip to Akron Children's no more than needed.

Chapter 4

Aplastic Anemia

A week later, Chris and I were on our way with Alayna back to the hospital. Dr. Fargo started the appointment doing his regular exam while the nurses took her blood. He then grabbed a stool and brought it in front of us, sitting down. He told us all of the biopsy results were in, and from what they could determine, Alayna's bone marrow was functioning at only 30%. Some places, even less.

"Aplastic Anemia," he explained. All my brain registered was the word anemia. In my head, I was thinking, shoot, this is nothing to worry about, an easy fix. The rest of that appointment was honestly a blur. Dr. Fargo seemed so calm, thoroughly explaining everything. I remember him telling us the disease was treatable, and one of the treatment options may be a bone marrow transplant. Bone marrow is spongy, fatty tissue in the center of your bones that produces red blood cells, white blood cells, and platelets. All of which were starting to fail Alayna.

A bone marrow transplant is a medical procedure used to replace damaged bone marrow. Bone marrow damage can be caused by several things, most often by disease, infection, and even certain type's chemotherapy. The transplant involves transplanting matched donated blood stem cells into your bloodstream. The cells then travel to the bone marrow, where they begin to produce more blood cells and promote growth in the new bone marrow.

Alayna's lab results came in right after, and of course, her platelet count was once again low. However, they were above 10,000, which meant no transfusion today. Her hemoglobin was beginning to take a plunge too. It wasn't anything of concern yet, but they were going to keep a close eye on it. Within the next week or so, she would most likely need a red blood transfusion. These results again confirmed everything they saw in the biopsy.

Dr. Fargo advised us to get Alayna's blood checked the following Monday at our local hospital. After, they will call us with her results and a plan of action if needed. Not long after he finished talking, a woman walked in. She introduced herself as Heather, one of the social workers at the hospital. She was super sweet and full of helpful knowledge about programs and what not that could with Alayna's diagnosis. She brought us a lunch box in the shade of Alayna's favorite color, purple. Inside was a 30-day free parking pass, coupons for the cafeteria, and goodies to keep us busy for the many upcoming appointments. She also recommended the lunch box for useful transportation of any medications Alayna may need in the future.

After Heather left, we got introduced to another woman named Courtney. She was a Nurse Practitioner as well as the Bone Marrow Transplant Coordinator. I was confused about why we would need to meet her so early when we were just given a diagnosis. They were quick to explain Courtney would be the one to help us find a bone marrow match if it came down to that treatment route. There were so many ifs, so much information all from one appointment. Everything was overwhelming, and I was struggling to process all of it.

It wasn't until the drive home that everything sunk in at once. I kept glancing at the paperwork the doctor had given us regarding Aplastic Anemia. Aplastic Anemia is the deficiency of all types of blood cells caused by the failure of the bone marrow production. An autoimmune disease where the body fails to produce sufficient numbers of blood cells. It is a remarkably rare disease, having only around 300-600 new cases across all age groups annually. It's a one-in-a-million disease, with no known causes in most cases. Very few, however, have been linked to pesticides. Alayna's case was severe. *Severe* Aplastic Anemia was the exact diagnosis on the paperwork. I explained all of this to Chris, reading aloud. It wasn't cancer, but the disease itself and the treatment options seemed very similar. Alayna did indeed have a life-threatening diagnosis.

Alayna was in good spirits when we arrived home, and began playing. Once again, I headed straight to the internet. Tons of information popped out at me. I began taking notes of any questions I had for her next appointment, based on what I was reading. The majority of it wasn't necessarily good, and to say the least, I was scared. Turning to Facebook, I began searching for an awareness group to reach out too. I found one and posted my story, in hopes of receiving positive experiences back. A friend had also reached out to us saying that her sister had been diagnosed with Aplastic Anemia, though a mild form, and is able to live a completely normal and healthy life. That made me feel better, but from what the doctors were telling us, I realized Alayna's case was not mild.

At the next appointment, Alayna's hemoglobin had dropped to around 7 which is low for a child. She needed a red blood transfusion. A red blood cell transfusion is a lot longer than a platelet transfusion. They normally take 4-6 hours.

From there, everything went downhill. Our weekly scheduled appointments ended up always being moved because Alayna's labs would be extremely low. She could never make it a complete whole week without blood or platelets. I had to stop working, as it was too stressful to find someone to watch Alayna or run Mikey to daycare while fearing he will pick up an illness and pass it to Alayna. It was crazy to think that just three weeks ago, she seemed completely fine, was she though? Just like that, her bone marrow started failing.

All of these appointments ran together. After the labs came back with counts low enough, and they always did, they would re-poke her and start a transfusion through an IV. It became so routine. I hated watching her get poked while trying to hold her down. Every time I asked if we could go straight to the IV because I knew her levels would be low enough. But, they said no, they needed to be sure, despite the fact I was always right. I was thinking how wonderful a port would be at this point so she didn't have to go through this every week.

Then the day came where they asked to check Mikey's blood to see if he would match Alayna's bone marrow if we decided on that treatment route. In all of my research, I had learned that the transplant could essentially cure Alayna with a small chance of relapse, whereas the medication route would again just send her into remission. When matching for a bone marrow transplant, they look at the HLA (human leukocyte antigen) typing, which has five genes. Each of those five genes has two different versions, called alleles. To have a perfect match, the donor would have to have ten matching alleles. While siblings have the highest chance at matching compared to a parent, Mikey's chances of a 10/10 match were only about 25%.

We were still hesitant on that route, but we all agreed that if Mikey was miraculously a match, it should be the route to take. However, I felt terrible having Mikey go through the testing process. On his end, there was no reason for him to get poked he was just fine. But it would help Alayna. He watched what the nurse was doing as they prepped his skin for the needle to draw blood. He handled it like a champ to be honest, although of course he did cry. I kept telling myself he is a baby he won't remember this. That slightly helped my guilt. We went through with the testing process, and it would be a few weeks until the results came in. Until we get that answer we didn't really talk any other treatment plans and just maintained with weekly transfusions.

Almost every other morning, I would go in to wake Alayna up and her pillowcase would have puddles of dry blood on it as her gums suddenly start to bleed or if she accidentally scratched herself in her sleep. This was blood she couldn't afford to lose.

My mom, grandma, step mother, and sister-in-law were wonderful in helping watch Mikey during the weekdays. Chris still had to work, as we didn't know what our future would look like at that point. I had felt like all of the pressure was on me to make sure everything was arranged and taken care of.

I tried to start somewhat of a routine. Monday's were our local hospital appointments for lab work since it was closer. Alayna became a champ at finger pokes and didn't shed a single tear. Then Akron Children's clinic would call and tell us the day we needed to come in. We tried our best to keep these appointments towards the end of the week so she would at least be good over the weekend. The appointments would take most of the day. During the clinic appointments, we would pass the time watching the movie *SING*. We saw that movie countless times, especially the part where Ash would sing since it was Alayna's favorite. After a transfusion, we would always have to wait an hour to make sure there were no reactions, luckily there never was and Alayna always responded well.

Sometimes when Alayna needed her weekly platelets, they were out. We would have to leave and come back up the next day. As a mom, I felt like I always went through every worst-case scenario in my head. I was terrified of having to leave the hospital with no platelets for Alayna. What if we had gotten into a car accident? I had to work to stop doing that since everything was out of my control at that point. I just had to roll with it and hope for the best.

It was so hard on those days to go home and have her try to just "take it easy". It was still summer, she wanted to be outside playing.

After about three weeks, we sat down once again with Dr. Fargo. As he was going over the labs, I cut him off. I asked if they had Mikey's results yet and if they knew if he was a match. Chris and I both knew the chances were slim, but I had this intuition. During my research for Alayna, I found out Mikey's birthday was the day after Aplastic Anemia Awareness week. It felt like a sign.

Dr. Fargo looked at Chris and me, smiling. "Mikey is a 10/10 perfect match!" My mouth dropped, and I started crying. Goosebumps covered my body. We finally had a good chance at making Alayna better. Mikey even has the same blood type as Alayna. With Mikey being a perfect match, Alayna's best chance of beating this disease was to go forward with the bone marrow transplant. Chris and I both agreed it should be the route to take. While this route was scary, we had to move forward, and we had to move forward fairly quickly.

* * *

There were many times I had to take breaks and step away to the bathroom to pull myself together. I refused to let Alayna see me sad. She was still just a three-year-old girl and needed to be treated like one, though it wasn't easy. She didn't like to be "tame" as I would call it. She loved to be outside, running around and jumping. She was allowed, but I was right beside her, making sure she didn't fall and hit her head. It made me so anxious.

If you are a mother, then you know exactly what I'm talking about, that feeling in your stomach before your heart drops to your feet.

There were many times Alayna got upset with me and said, "Mommy, I'm fine. I am a big girl." She got annoyed with me, but I dealt with it. This is what I had to do to protect her. Alayna is a sassy, independent toddler and knows exactly what she wants. That attitude was exactly what she needed to get through this.

Chris and I lost sleep trying to research the best hospital for Alayna's treatment. We leaned on the support groups on Facebook to learn more of other's stories. It gave us the perspective of not forgetting how severe this disease is. Anyone with Severe Aplastic Anemia does not look sick on the outside so it's hard to understand. It was hard enough for us to grasp onto, let alone trying to tell others just how severe it is. I remember reading stories of kids who took the transplant route and passed away because they got an infection, and their body couldn't fight it. Or, in some cases, they survive the transplant but have complications a few years later. The thought of losing your child is unbearable. The thought of losing your child because of your choice in treatment is ten times worse. Just the possibility of losing her devastated us.

"What if she didn't make it because she got an infection? Would she be transfusion-dependent her whole life? How long can one survive with so many transfusions? What kind of life would that be like?" I asked these questions to myself countless times. Let alone, the other thing that really ate at me was it being idiopathic. So, they couldn't prove an exact cause for her Aplastic Anemia. It was mentally taking a toll on me.

We made a phone call to a doctor our insurance company had given us who actually specialized in Aplastic Anemia. He is located in Wisconsin and is extremely knowledgeable of the disease. Everyone on our support groups talked highly of him and his care. Of course, it went straight to his voicemail and I prepared myself to leave a proper message. After leaving him a voicemail I figured it would probably be at least a couple of days to a week before we heard anything from his office. I just sat there staring at Alayna thinking how terrible life can really be, then the phone rang. It was him! He called us back within a few minutes. When he started talking I don't think Chris and I ever paid more attention in any single conversation with anybody ever. I mean, this is our first-born baby we were talking about here. He was very helpful in helping guide us and making sure we knew and understood all of the treatment options. I originally just said well let's pack our bags and head to Wisconsin and have Alayna do her treatment there. It wouldn't be that simple though as he recommends all of his patients from out of town stay close by for at least 6 months to assure proper care.

As easy of a decision you think it would be to say yes, it's a very hard decision when you have more children involved and a household that needs upkeep. Chris still had to work or there was no way the bills would get paid. I know mentally that I wouldn't be able to handle being on my own. I praise those parents who have to make that tough decision and one has to stay behind.

Chapter 5

Admission

* August *

August came, and so did endless appointments. During one of them, a doctor from the transplant team at Akron Children's joined us, Dr. Sampson. We talked about the process of a bone marrow transplant and all of the possible scenarios that could occur. It was hard to listen to. All of the medicines she would take had tons of potential unsettling side effects. One of those medications needed to prepare her for the transplant was Chemotherapy. It would be a reduced intensity regimen of chemotherapy, meaning it would be a lesser version of Chemo and not as intense. Either way you look at it though, it's chemotherapy. Not only would Alayna lose her hair, but she also would have the slim possibility of not being able to have children of her own. Hearing that just devastated me even more. I just know that when she is older, if she happens to have any complications with conceiving a child, she will know and understand our decision-making process for her.

During the same appointment, we took a tour of the Ronald McDonald House. Alayna would be in the hospital for a month post-transplant, and we would have to live within 10 minutes of the hospital for 100 days after in case any complications arose. The Ronald McDonald House is a place for families to stay close to their hospitalized children. It would serve as a perfect home for us during those 100 days, for little to no money.

Before we left the hospital, they encouraged us to get a second opinion on Alayna's treatment as we were still debating on which hospital. When we got home later that day, Chris and I looked up the top hospitals based on what the doctors have told us. We got an appointment scheduled with Cincinnati Children's Hospital and met with a doctor down there. The doctor recommended all of the same treatments that Akron Children's did. Since Mikey was a perfect match, the doctor agreed that the transplant was the best chance to give Alayna a full recovery and a long, healthy life.

Based on Alayna's counts, they suggested going through with the transplant within the next three weeks. This was a shock to hear because we had originally talked about October, that is why we were taking our time with researching hospitals. However, Alayna's body wasn't stable enough to even go forward with the transplant. Alayna's body was failing her. To the point where her immune system was nothing. All of her blood counts were extremely low. She became neutropenic, meaning she was very vulnerable to any type of infection. There was a high chance of her catching a minor illness and her body not being able to fight it. We were constantly on the lookout for fevers or signs of sickness. With such low counts and a high risk of infection, she needed to stay away from the public there on out. We started wearing masks during her appointments and tried to keep her at home as often as we could.

We began giving her a daily Neupogen shot to help boost her levels and get them to a safe range to proceed with the transplant. At one of her appointments they had Chris and I practice injecting an orange. It's one thing to have to hold your child down so a nurse can inject her with a shot once a week but, for the parents to have to administer a shot daily for a 3-year-old was just heart wrenching to say the least. It was not easy but had to be done to give Alayna the best chance possible at having a successful transplant. She also started taking antifungal medicine three times a day. The cost of both of them was over $700. After they prescribed it for us, I went in to pick it up. I was shocked when they told me the cost.

Alayna had gotten so used to being poked that whenever we played hospital, she would take everyone's blood and give them shots. It broke my heart to watch. She was just an innocent little girl who didn't understand the dangerous disease she had. "It will hurt for just a few seconds," she would tell her patients. While she seemed like a typical three-year-old on the outside, the inside was the complete opposite.

Chris and I had long conversations about the pros and cons of each hospital we looked into and what would be best for our family. In the end, we decided to go through with the transplant locally and continue her care through Akron Children's. The staff there knew us and our situation, not to mention, they got along with Alayna great. We felt more of a family sense with them, Alayna wouldn't just be another patient.

* September *

September came and brought an admission date of the 16th. At one of our appointments, they gave us a folder of all of the medications used during the transplant. I had to read over each page and initial my understanding and bring it back to our transplant meeting the following week. Chris couldn't look at it. I couldn't even begin to describe how difficult it was to read each page and its' horrific contents. I could lose my daughter to these medicines because of a choice I made, and it was killing me.

I am a natural-born planner. I always need a clear path to go forward, but at that point, I couldn't plan ahead. I couldn't see what Alayna's future would hold or how it would affect us. I had to learn to take things day by day.

Before Alayna could go through with the transplant, they had to wipe out what was remaining of her immune system. It was crazy to think that we were trying to get her levels to a safe range for them to just wipe it out again to condition her body for the transplant. After a full recovery, they would start to revaccinate her. There would be so much medicine going into a teeny tiny body. It was scary to think of all the ways it could affect her.

The second week into September, we met with the staff of the transplant team. Before coming in for the meeting, Alayna and Mikey went through pre-testing. We literally went all over the hospital that day. One of the tests for Mikey was genetic-based, the doctors needed to make sure the disease didn't pass through genes. If it did, we would have to change our entire treatment route since Mikey's bone marrow could potentially act the same as Alayna's. That was an unsettling thought to have. Right before our meeting we were able to meet with a wonderful woman who gave us hope, her name was Alexis. She brought Alayna a unicorn pillow with a blanket inside. It was such a nice gesture. Alexis' son had a bone marrow transplant at Akron Children's two years ago for the same exact disease Alayna had. She had mentioned how her son is thriving and Alayna will breeze right through everything. She was so sweet to talk to and I greatly appreciated her for taking the time out of her day to meet with us, though it was brief with all of the pre-testing appointments.

The transplant meeting soon came, it was tough sitting down with the staff. I felt like I was going to vomit from the nerves of everything. I remember Chris looking at Dr. Kuerbitz, who was taking over Alayna's case and said, "I couldn't read over that medication list. Thinking about it is too hard. I'm going to rely on you guys, you're the experts."

"Yes, that's definitely not an easy matter to talk about," Dr. Kuerbitz replied with a pitying smile.

The meeting went on, and they answered any questions we had. We also met with the palliative care team, which made me even more nauseous. They had explained that in some severe cases, children can develop sores not only in their mouth but all through their esophagus and digestive system from the chemotherapy and it can be very painful. If Alayna were to have this side effect, they would make sure she is as comfortable as possible. This was going to be a tough road ahead for Alayna. I just had to stop thinking about the "what if's" and embrace the positives in the current situation. Once we felt satisfied with the information they had for us, we signed the paper officially allowing the transplant to happen. In return, they handed us a calendar outlining Alayna's conditioning regimen up until the day of the transplant. It found a home on our refrigerator as a reminder and countdown of what was to come. It was crazy to think that in just a week, we would be living in the hospital. I kept telling myself that this was the best chance Alayna had.

I had never been a very religious person. I believed in God, but I never went to church. Growing up, I dealt with a couple of deaths in my family. They were hard to accept. I didn't understand why God would put someone through that pain. Even now, I felt like I was being punished in some way. But I started praying. I asked others to pray. At this point, it was all up to God with the help of the medical professionals.

To help raise support for Alayna, I had rubber bracelets made. They were purple, her favorite color, and had our motto, "AlaynaStrong", on it. We were shocked at how many people bought one. The money we brought in helped our financial situation and kept the bills paid. We ended up getting a lot of donations, too. My dad and brother's work went above and beyond and gave us a very generous donation. During their lunch break, I went to thank them all.

I remember standing there as my brother was talking to everyone. Hearing his kind words towards his niece made me break down. I fought with everything to keep it in, but it was something I had no control over. He was talking about my baby girl, the one I created. Why was this happening to her, to our family?

The rest of the week, we prepared to be away for four months. I cleared the cupboards and fridge of foods that would spoil while we were away. Family came over for last-minute going away visits as long as they were healthy. If Mikey or Alayna fell sick now, the transplant would get postponed. We were so close. We just had to make it a couple more days.

One day at lunch, Alayna was sitting on a stool at the counter. She slipped before I could grab her. She fell, hitting her chin. It immediately began to bruise badly and swell. We were beyond lucky she didn't hit her head and had received platelets the day before. I called the hospital to get their verdict, and they said she should be fine, as long as she didn't show any signs of a concussion. She thankfully never did.

Alayna had a final bone marrow biopsy to confirm nothing had miraculously changed. Chris and I handled it better this time, however, it was still hard seeing her lay there. It took a little longer for her to wake up. The nurse in the room with us explained some kids pop right up, while others wake up slowly. Less than ten seconds later, Alayna literally popped right up. We all shared a good laugh, which was a nice change from my usual worrying.

September 15th, 2019, the day we left our normal life behind had come. My emotions were racing. I was relieved we were heading in the right direction, but I was also worried about what this direction would bring. I dropped our cat, Max, and our dog, Rico, off to my mother's house the night before. They would stay with her until we were able to come back home. Josie, our other dog, would stay with our neighbors.

I spent the morning packing and making sure Alayna had everything she would need. We only lived about forty minutes away, so we could drive home when we needed to. While I was packing, Chris was preparing to take Josie to the neighbors. I gave Josie a big hug with tears rolling down my face. Everything seemed like a dream up until now.

Shortly after, my mom came to pick up Mikey. She was going to watch him for a night or two, so our focus could be on Alayna and helping her through her chemo since we didn't know how she would respond to it. It was so hard to Mikey goodbye, Mommy will see you in a couple of days. I gave him a giant hug before closing the car door. As I watched my mom drive away down the drive way, I remember turning around and going back inside to a seemingly empty house and just let it all out. I dropped on my knees in the kitchen and started bawling like a baby. It was such a relief to just let it all out I can't even tell you how good it actually felt. All of the emotions were coming to me, sad, scared, happy and mad. You name it, I felt it that day. I needed that cry.

Alayna was waiting for me on the couch in the living room. I pulled myself together again. I went to sit with her and just held her. We had tried to prepare her for this as best as we could, but it was hard. We had been telling that her blood was not healthy and that Mikey is going to share some of his blood with her. While her blood is getting healthy, she will have to stay in the hospital. She also knew she would lose her hair, but that it would grow back. A couple of days ago, a friend of mine offered to cut Alayna's hair short for free, so it wouldn't be a surprise when she started losing it.

I wish the moment Alayna and I had on the couch could have lasted forever. We were already behind schedule and running late but I didn't care, this was our last 'normal' day for a while.

We had to get on the road to check into the Ronald McDonald House. Alayna would then go to the hospital to receive blood and platelets to make sure her levels were safe for her Broviac surgery the next morning. A Broviac is a port with a central line going into her bloodstream that allows long term access. I was beyond excited for this because Alayna wouldn't need IV's to get her medicine anymore.

After we checked in, we rushed over to the hospital. It was already near 4:00 pm, and her transfusions would take five hours to complete. It would be late by the time we finally got out. The nurses were trying to persuade us to stay the night, but I said no, wanting one last night together as a family. I left for our room about six hours later, wanting to shower and unpack our things. Walking through the door, a wave of nerves and stress about the future hit me. I wasn't mentally prepared for what Alayna was about to go through. I got in the shower and cried. I felt like showers were the only time I had to myself, my only chance to let go of all the emotions I was holding in. After I felt slightly better, I got out and watched television until Chris brought Alayna back around midnight. We all climbed into bed together and fell fast asleep.

A short five hours later, we began waking up and got ready to head to the hospital as Alayna needed to be checked in by 6am. Once Alayna was checked in, they took us to a room with a curtain. Alayna was in good spirits despite not getting a full night's rest. Taking our chance, we began to explain to her she wouldn't be able to leave the hospital for a while. She understood as we had prepared her well. The nurses in the room with us were amazed at how smart and understanding she was for her age.

Within a couple of minutes, an anesthesiologist and a nurse walked in. They took their notes over Alayna, asking us a couple of questions before walking out. Right after, the surgeon came in and gave us a brief rundown of the procedure. A child life specialist came in right after, holding an assortment of flavored chap sticks. She let Alayna choose her favorite flavor, telling her she will rub it on her mask. Alayna picked out the orange flavoring, and then they practiced breathing through the mask. After Alayna mastered the art of breathing through the mask, she took Alayna's hand and led her to a group of push-cars. Alayna picked out a red car. Before we knew it, they were ready. Alayna was not. When she found out Chris and I couldn't go back with her, she burst into tears. I could see the fear in her eyes. Ignoring the tears rolling down my face, we assured her we weren't leaving and would be right beside her when she woke up.

As the nurse pushed the car down the hallway towards the operating room, Alayna looked back, reaching out, screaming, "Mommy, Mommy!" The doors closing behind her, she swallowed her cries. I turned to Chris, and he held me as we both cried. It wasn't fair. All of this had happened within eight weeks. Eight weeks ago, we were having the greatest night of our lives. Two days later, our lives flipped upside down. Eight weeks ago, everything was in my control. Now, everything was going to be in the hands of the medical team on Unit 5600.

We made our way back to the surgical waiting area. Thirty nerve-wrenching minutes later, they updated us with the start of the procedure. They reported that Alayna had a rough start without us, but quickly calmed down. A little over an hour had passed before the surgery was finally over. Everything went amazing. As we made our way to recovery, I heard Alayna's little cry. Her voice was hoarse from the intubation. She finally came into sight, her head buried in a nurse's shoulder. She settled down once she saw us, and soon, she was in and out of sleep. She was in some pain, her throat hurt the most. Her vitals were great, however, so we didn't stay in recovery for long. Before long, we were on our way to her new room for the next month.

Room 5653. Waiting for us in the room was our RN, Mandy. I took to her right away, she was full of knowledge on bone marrow transplants and helped calm me down.

The rest of the day was pretty laid back. Alayna was sore and groggy, so she took it easy. Nick and Bre came up and visited with us for a while. Alayna wasn't necessarily in isolation, she couldn't leave her room, but she could have visitors as long as no one was sick. Chris and I agreed to limit Alayna's exposure to people since we didn't want to chance her catching any illnesses. We only allowed our immediate family to visit occasionally, and we treated it like isolation.

Sitting to the side, watching Alayna lay down, I decided to start a journal. Every day I would write in it to give updates on how Alayna was feeling. I thought it would be something for her to look back on when she is older as it would help keep track of what happened, especially on the days I was upset. Not only did it help me keep things straight, but it was also therapeutic for me to fuel my emotions into the writing. Thus, is how my idea came to make it into a book to share with others.

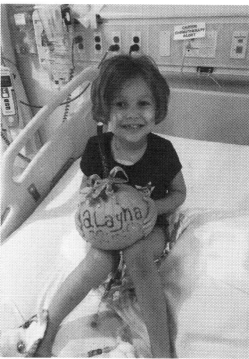

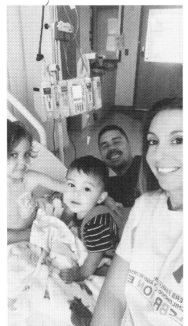
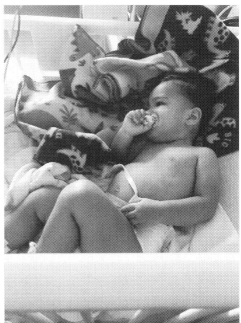
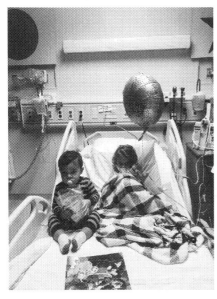

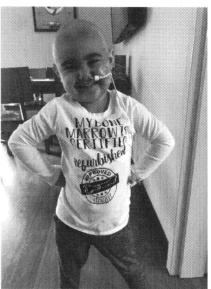

Chapter 6

Transplant

* Tuesday, September 17th, 2019 *

Day-7. The countdown until the transplant had officially begun. Here we are, literally 8 weeks later from the day we were given a diagnosis. Today, Alayna would begin the start of her chemotherapy. The transplant would take place in a week. I was a ball of nerves. The only major side effects, if any, the doctors expected for today were diarrhea or nausea. Of course, hair loss happens but that is usually 1-2 weeks Alayna woke up in a playful mood, which made me feel slightly better about the situation. I just wasn't ready for my baby to take chemo and go through everything it entails. It's every parent's worst nightmare.

Alayna's first dose would begin around 4 pm. The round of chemotherapy medication she is starting is called Fludarabine. It will be given through her Broviac. She would get four doses of it total, and today was her first dosage. After a long morning of running around, Alayna crashed. She slept through the entire administration, which was a relief.

Today we also started a very strict mouth and skin care routine as well as a Metabolic Diet. For the mouth care, Alayna needed to rinse her mouth with a Biotene rinse 3 times a day. Since she still hasn't gotten the hang of spitting yet, I dip a mouth swab in the Biotene and rub it around inside her mouth. The Biotene is supposed to help with dry mouth and help with pain as the Chemo can cause mouth sores. As for the skin care, Alayna will need wiped down with CHG wipes once a day as well as her usual bath. The CHG wipes (short for Chlorhexidine) is a wipe that kills germs. A daily wipe down with a CHG wipe can help reduce the spread of infections as Alayna's immunity is getting completely wiped out so a small scratch could have to potential to create a severe infection. The metabolic diet is anything that is opened or cooked, must be eaten within one hour. After an hour, if needs to be thrown away as bacteria starts to grow. Too much bacteria can cause Alayna to get super sick. We also changed Alayna's bedding once a day.

Chris and I took turns each night sleeping with Alayna at the hospital. The other would go back and sleep with Mikey at the Ronald McDonald House.

* Wednesday, September 18th, 2019 *

Day -6. Alayna woke up full of energy and silliness. She was smiles and giggles all day long. She took all of her medications by mouth without any complaints. I decided she earned a reward, and I got her Orbeez. For weeks, she had been begging me to get her some. After endless searching, I finally found some I was able to pick up at Target. She had a fantastic time playing with them.

She ended up eating well, too. Sometimes it can be a struggle to get her to eat all of her food, especially if it is something she dislikes. She got her second dose of Fludarabine around 4 pm again. This time around, she began to feel ill as she received the medicine. The nurse gave her Zofran and another medicine I didn't catch the name of to prevent nausea.

With all of the medicine in her system, she shortly fell fast asleep. After a refreshing nap, she was back on her feet in a few hours. The medicine kept her from feeling ill, so she was in good spirits once again. With all these late naps, Alayna is not settling down until 12 or 1 am. Kelsey is our night nurse, it was so good to see her again. She surprisingly remembered us from when Alayna was first admitted in July.

* Thursday, September 19th, 2019 *

Day -5. We were getting closer and closer to Day 0, transplant day. Part of me was so ready but at the same time still wasn't. Alayna, on the other hand, was doing fantastic. She was given her third dose of the Fludarabine, and she did wonderfully. She was quite the little trooper! Her mood remained high and silly. She continued to take all of her medicines without fault. She had become quite the night owl since her late naps had her staying up later and later. I wasn't complaining as long as she stayed in a great mood. We were so proud of our strong, little girl.

* Friday September 20th, 2019 *

Day -4. Despite how well Alayna had been doing, I was still a nervous wreck for what was to come, today especially. Alayna was going to begin ATG therapy today. ATG stands for anti-thymocyte globulin. It is an infusion of rabbit or horse derived antibodies against human T-lymphocytes. It is most commonly used in organ transplants, but also as a treatment option for aplastic anemia. Alayna will get one dose of ATG daily for three days. The unknown of how her body would react to the new medicine was scary. A lot was being put into her tiny body. My only hope was that she could handle it without any problems. I had stayed with Mikey the night prior so when we got to the hospital the next morning, the doctors had already done their morning rounds and check-up. Our RN today was Mandy, which was a huge relief. She explained she would stay in the room mostly throughout the day as Alayna will need to be monitored every 15-20 minutes. My mind was blanking from the nerves, and I couldn't remember any of the side effects of the new medicines. Concerned, I asked Mandy if she was able to explain the possible side effects of it. She very calmly explained to me that high blood pressure could occur, along with a fever and chills.

My eyes filled with tears. In my head, I was replaying a memory of something one of the transplant doctors had said to me when we had talked about a bone marrow transplant as an option. She told me there had been cases in the past when the blood pressure went out of control. The children had to be taken into the intensive care unit (ICU) until it was stable. I wasn't too concerned with it back then, but now it was a real possibility. Mandy reassured me they were prepared for anything, and if anything were to happen, they have all proper medications on standby. Along with the ATG, Alayna had her fourth and final dose of Fludarabine. She went to bed at a decent time for the first time in days, as well.

* Saturday, September 21, 2019 *

Day -3. Today was another day filled with lots of medicine. Alayna received her second dose of ATG treatment. Along with it, she began another chemotherapy called Cyclophosphamide. She will also start a new medication called Cyclosporine. Cyclophosphamide is chemotherapy used to suppress the immune system, and cyclosporine is an immunosuppressant drug that will help the body not reject the new bone marrow that will be introduced. Rejection of the new marrow would result in Graft Versus Host Disease, or GVHD. GVHD can occur at any time after a transplant although it is more common to develop after the marrow has started to make healthy cells. The condition can vary from mild to severe. Some of the symptoms from it could be abdominal pain, diarrhea, dry eyes, rashes or weight loss. The doctors will start to monitor Alayna for this very closely. A person who has gone through an organ transplant has to be on Cyclosporine for the rest of their lives, but with bone marrow, it is the complete opposite. Doctors have yet to figure out why, but with a bone marrow transplant, you only have to be on Cyclosporine for around a year, sometimes longer. The body eventually accepts the new marrow over time, whereas with an organ transplant, any missed dosages could result in the body rejecting the organ. Alayna responded to everything great, once again. Since she was doing so well, and Mandy was still monitoring her, she encouraged Chris and I to leave for dinner and would call us if she needed to. Alayna was fine with it. We took Mikey and ate dinner together at the Ronald McDonald House. I needed a break, and it was nice to get one. However, it was sad that my break was a family dinner. It's crazy how you take small things like that for granted.

* Sunday, September 22, 2019 *

Day -2. It was a rather uneventful day. Alayna had her last dosages of ATG and Cyclophosphamide. She has been taking Zofran daily to keep her nausea away, which has helped a lot. She does seem to tire easily but she was in a playful mood, and I was very thankful. These medicines could be bringing her down, but she has handled it amazingly. She is one strong little girl. I, on the other hand, have stressed myself out to the max trying to keep Mikey healthy. Only two more days. I can't even imagine if he were to get sick how this would affect everything. My worst nightmare used to be something like this happening to one of the children. And now I was living it. Now, my worst nightmare had become the possibility of either Mikey or Alayna falling sick. I couldn't imagine how it could affect everything. Tomorrow, Mikey would go in for the harvest of his bone marrow. I wasn't as nervous as I was with Alayna, but it was still scary. He was so young, only a mere one year old. You just never know how someone will respond to anesthesia. I had to keep reminding myself to take it one day at a time.

* Monday, September 23, 2019 *

Day -1. Today was Alayna's rest day before the big day. She had finished all of her conditioning treatments, so her only medicines were the regular ones she took orally, as well as her Cyclosporine. My mom drove up to stay with Alayna, so Chris and I could be with Mikey during his surgery. His harvest began in the afternoon. Like Alayna, Mikey got to pick out his own car before heading back to the operating room. He picked blue and of course, had to drive around while he was waiting to go back. I handled it a little better than I expected. He's a tough little boy.

I remember when we first found out Mikey was a match, we got a lot of judgmental questions, asking if we should put Mikey through this, and it upset me. I would never want my child to go through any pain or harm. But at the same time, I know my child. He is young, but he is strong. He won't remember this and I know it will bring him and Alayna even closer as they grow up together. Without Mikey as a match, who knows where Alayna would be right now. Most likely, she would be sitting on the registry list, waiting for a match as her body failed her. It is sad to think of all the kids who desperately need a bone marrow transplant, or any type of transplant, but don't have a matched donor. That is why signing up is so important. I had never really thought twice about it before, unfortunately. I am happy to say I know a couple of people who have signed up since Alayna got diagnosed. Alayna's story had opened the eyes of others on why donating is so important. It is giving my daughter a second chance to live freely.

Mikey went through surgery just fine. I was nervous, but I knew he could handle it. When we got back to recovery, he was pretty fussy, but I held him and rocked him. I felt terrible for putting him through this. But we knew this was the only way to help his sister. They were able to get a room for Mikey right next to Alayna's. He would have to stay overnight just for observation since it was his first time under anesthesia. They also wanted to make sure his hemoglobin was regenerating properly. The doctors came in to let us know everything went great, and they got all of the marrow they needed without any problems. The marrow was on its way to Cincinnati for processing and testing. Once we got to the room, Mikey was groggy and sore. But he ate all of his chicken broth for Grammy, which was a good sign.

Chris and I, unfortunately, were not having much luck. We both had to go over with Alayna has her Broviac dressing needed changed. It gets changed weekly, sooner if it gets wet. It was like a big sticker that was covering the line to keep out germs as well as holding it in place. We had to hold her down for that as she screamed. Then when we thought the worst was over the doctors decided to insert an NG feeding tube today out of all days as the mouth sores could potentially start to develop from the chemo causing Alayna to not want to eat. She had no signs of them luckily but they wanted to be prepared for them. Alayna also has to drink a ton of fluids due to the daily medicine she is taking so this would be a good way to get the extra fluid in. I had to hold Alayna down on top of me, while the other nurses held her arms and legs down. Meanwhile, another nurse was shoving a tube down her nose into her stomach.

It was terrible. I never want her to have to go through something like that again. I know Chris was not happy at all about it, though he soon did realize that it had to be done for precautionary reasons.

Afterward, Alayna got incredibly sick and couldn't stop vomiting which wasn't good because she could vomit the tube up, having to re insert it. It was hard to watch her go from feeling 'okay and comfortable' to 'vomiting profusely and being so uncomfortable.' I have never wanted to be in two places at once more than I did at that moment. I felt torn. Both of my kids didn't feel good. It was hard to see her go from being comfortable and ok to vomiting and crying. I am so grateful my mom was able to stay and help with Mikey. I barely saw him after his surgery and the guilt was setting in. After we were able to get Alayna settled with no more vomiting, I slept in Mikey's room to keep an eye on him. He was calm the entire night, it was almost as if he knew he was helping his sister. Our little hero!

* Tuesday, September 24, 2019 *

Day 0. It was finally Transplant Day! Alayna was not feeling well at all today. To lighten the mood, I went to the hospital's gift shop and bought Alayna balloons to celebrate with. Nerves were eating away every part of me, but I had to put on a brave face for my daughter. Mikey felt completely back to normal. He doesn't have to take any medicine except for a daily vitamin to build his iron back up.

Bre had come up and stayed for a while to help my mom with Alayna as Mikey was released so Chris and I were able to get him settled back at the Ronald McDonald House for a nap. We all needed a mental break after everything we witnessed with Alayna yesterday. I felt guilty because she can't leave and is stuck in her room. After resting for a while, we brought Mikey back to the hospital. A few hours later, the bone marrow had been received back from the hospital in Cincinnati. Courtney brought it in to show us, Mikey and Alayna got their pictures taken together with it. It warmed my heart seeing both of their names written on it, knowing that it was the key to healing my daughter. Courtney was the one who administered the bone marrow through Alayna's Broviac. It fell with the gravity, and Alayna endured it well. By 3:40pm, the transplant was officially underway, and Alayna had been rebirthed! It was her second chance at life, after all.

Chapter 7

A New Beginning

* Wednesday, September 25, 2019 *

Day +1. Alayna was overall doing good. She spent the day exhausted and sad from everything that has happened. It is all beginning to catch up with her, and that is a lot for a three-year-old to comprehend. We didn't do much today, Alayna spent most of her day in bed.

Thursday, September 26, 2019 *

Day +2. Alayna began to fight sleep. She was tired yet again as a result of it. However, on the bright side, she managed to eat a little more than normal, which was fantastic.

* Friday, September 27, 2019 *

Day +3. Alayna's eating has been better, and she was drinking fluids well. The doctors decided to take Alayna off of fluids and her tube feed for the morning and afternoon. She was up walking around and playing, which I was glad to see. Seeing her free without tubes hanging in her way brought a smile to my face. So far, she hasn't had any setbacks, which was excellent news. I hope she continues to do so great.

* Saturday, September 28, 2019 *

Day +4. Alayna's energy didn't flow into today, however. She must have overdone it yesterday. She was run down and not feeling well. We made sure to keep fluids in her, hoping it will make her feel better.

* Sunday, September 29, 2019 *

Day +5. Alayna woke up well-rested and looking a lot better. She is just very run-down and overall, quite sad. I hated seeing her like this, it is far from her regular energy. There is still no sign of engraftment of Mikey's cells, but it is still very early. The doctors said she was doing fantastic so far.

* Wednesday, October 2, 2019 *

Day +8. Alayna's cells began to engraft already. It was great news considering it has been just over a week since the transplant. Her ANC, absolute neutrophil count, is close to 300. The ANC is basically her immunity, and previously, her count was 0. I was happy to finally see numbers on her lab results.

The doctors were having a hard time trying to find the right dosage of Cyclosporine to give her. So far, it had been on the lower end of the range, but they want her levels up, so it needed to be increased. Unfortunately, she had to take the awful medication by mouth because it is super sticky. If they put it in her NG tube, it would stick to the plastic. All of the other medicines she had been taking through her NG, which was one good thing about it. I was on the lookout for mouth sores, and so far, there hadn't been any signs.

* Friday, October 4, 2019 *

Day +10. There had yet to be any setbacks, Alayna was doing fantastic. Her levels were steady, and the doctors said we could hopefully be released within the next two weeks. She, unfortunately, developed a minor blood pressure issue. Her doctors were working on finding the right dosage of medicine to control it. They assumed it was a side effect from the Cyclosporine.

At one point, her blood pressure soared so high they had to give her what they called a rescue medication. The highest her blood pressure got was 140/100. That was high for an adult, let alone a toddler. It was scary to see it so high, but I tried to keep calm. If she got worked up, she could send it even higher. Other than that small blip, our day was good. I noticed a couple of strands of hair falling out, which was the first of many, sadly.

* Saturday, October 5, 2019 *

Day +11. When Alayna woke up, it seemed as if all of her hair decided to fall out overnight. Her pillow was covered, and it was making a mess everywhere. It stuck on every surface possible, including her mouth. She almost had a meltdown before I swooped in and helped her clear her mouth out. By tomorrow, she will have officially engrafted all of her new cells from Mikey. Complete engraftment happens when they see ANC levels of at least 500 for three consecutive days.

* Sunday, October 6, 2019 *

Day +12. Alayna has officially engrafted all of Mikey's cells. Her hair was still falling out, getting stuck in her mouth, and making a mess. Chris stayed with Alayna tonight while I was in the Ronald McDonald House with Mikey. He decided to cut her hair and sent me a picture of it. Bald spots were showing, and it was very uneven. It didn't seem to help much however, she was still shedding. We planned on trying to shave it tomorrow.

* Monday, October 7, 2019 *

Day +13. All was still well. She didn't have any fevers or mouth sores like anticipated. The doctors were amazed by how well she was doing. We did end up shaving the rest of her hair off as we planned. She didn't like the noise, but she braved through it. To finish it off, I took a lint roller over it to catch all of the little hairs that were remaining. Alayna made a cute little bald girl.

As I was walking to the kitchen to make an Easy Mac for Alayna (Easy Mac's were an everyday thing, but at least she was eating), I overheard one of the doctors talking with a nurse about a patient. She told the nurse to let the family know that they did think it was cancer, but they had to do further testing. I felt my heart break. I wanted to go find the family and the child and hold them. Knowing that another family received the most devastating news of their lives made me cry. I knew all too well the emotions they would soon be feeling.

* From Then On *

I decided to stop my daily updates for the rest of our stay. Not only was I bad at remembering, thankfully there weren't any significant changes to report. Alayna was still doing really well and never got mouth sores or fevers. She got one platelet transfusion, but other than that, she was doing fantastic. It felt like she breezed right through everything. I was on edge, waiting for a setback. I knew better than to think like that, but I couldn't help it.

There was so much talk of the setbacks that could and most likely would happen. After all she had been through, it seemed inevitable. The doctors had prepared us for the worst.

I knew she still had a long way to go, but Alayna was rocking this. I still feared she would develop an infection that her body couldn't fight off. But her labs looked amazing, there didn't seem to be any chance of her crashing down. Of course, she still had no immune system but it was crazy seeing close to somewhat normal blood levels after months of dangerously low numbers. Every day I prayed there wouldn't be any setbacks.

As I mentioned before, her sticker covering her Broviac gets changed every couple of days to prevent infection, it's horrible. She lays on me and again I have to hold her down while they peel off the sticker and clean around the Broviac. She is just petrified of everything at this point. I felt horrible helping the nurses do this to her when all she wants is her mommy to hold her and tell her it is okay. I try my best to keep her calm, but I wished I didn't have to do this to her. I wanted to trade places with her, and I would've in a heartbeat.

She still took steroids as part of her medications, and let me tell you, roid rage is real. Alayna has always been sassy, but lately, I felt as if I didn't know who she was. She was moody and mean to everybody, despite us repeatedly telling her we were only trying to help. She kicked her bedside table over, which was completely unlike her. I couldn't wait for her to get off of them. They affected her physically too. Looking back at pictures to compare, she had gotten quite swollen from the steroids. She looked like a completely different child.

We passed time with different therapies. Occupational therapy and physical therapy came in daily. Alayna also had art and music therapy, which were her favorites. We danced and sang and drew on her dry erase board. One of the walls in her room is entirely dry erase. Of course, we watched SING still. I was surprised it was still on the rotation of movies, they seem to change every few months.

Despite how much we loved her doctors and nurses, we were on a floor no parent wanted their child on. It was hard listening to your child scream in the middle of the night because the nurses woke them up to take vitals. But hearing someone else's child scream through the walls was even harder. I felt so bad, I wanted to personally go in and comfort each child, one by one. There was something special about being on that floor, though. It changes you. It is full of courage and hope. It was admirable how resilient and tough the kids who reside on that floor are. This floor taught me to stop, and take care of myself, so I am strong enough to care for Alayna and Mikey to the best of my abilities.

Before we were admitted to the hospital, I told myself I would try to reach out to other families, so I did. Two other children were going through bone marrow transplants at the same time as us. They both had cancer. Us parents tried to check in with each other when we could to see how our little fighters were doing. I almost didn't want to report Alayna's good news because their children weren't so lucky. They both had setbacks, but they both had Chemotherapy before their transplant. Alayna's first time was right before her transplant. The toll it takes on their little bodies is crazy. Again, I was moved by the bravery and strength of all the children on that floor.

The hospital offered us massages. They were a nice escape from reality for a while. We also got monthly dinners, it was nice to eat something that wasn't from the cafeteria without spending money. Chris and I had begun to worry about being able to pay the bills with the both of us not working. My cousin Heather does marketing and event planning. I asked her for her thoughts on hosting a benefit dinner for Alayna. I hated asking for help, but I was scared of what these bills would turn into. There were a couple of organizations and foundations that helped us, but since Alayna doesn't have cancer, she doesn't qualify for a lot of them.

My family worked their butts off to pull off a benefit for us while Alayna was in the hospital. There was a ton of advertising, gathering, and planning to do, but they did it. They talked to tons of companies and got over 85 donated baskets for a basket raffle and silent auction. There were corn-hole tournaments, poker, and special item drawings. They also managed to get a donated rigatoni dinner. Chris and I were hoping to bring in enough to cover the costs of anything we had to pay for out of pocket. We never expected as much as we got.

The benefit turned out beyond amazing and brought in so much for us. We were told over 400 people showed up, not counting everybody my family enlisted to help with different tasks. We are so thankful for our family, friends, and community. It's crazy how such a small little girl could have such a huge impact on so many people. We are and always will be forever grateful for everyone who donated their time, effort, and money into our cause. Chris and I were overwhelmed when we were told the outcome. Chris' sister Michelle and her husband Jonathan, also held a fundraiser for us at her place of employment in California. We are truly blessed and thankful to all of the kind hearts who helped our daughter.

Chapter 8

Goodbye Hospital

* October *

After 31 days in the hospital, Alayna was released early from the hospital on October 17th. She gets to say with us at the Ronald McDonald House across the street. Twice a week, however, she would go back for clinic appointments. I was nervous but beyond excited for all of us to be under one roof again. We were definitely prepared. Our rooms were unpacked and put together, awaiting Alayna's arrival. Still, some part of me was afraid something would go wrong. Chris and I were taught how to administer all of Alayna's medications and tube feeds. She had to have an intake of 2,000 mL of fluid each day.

We learned how to flush her Broviac, which we had to do once a day.

Next week, her Broviac will come out and get replaced with a port that goes underneath her skin. It will be nice to bathe her without having to worry about her Broviac getting wet. I also worried she would get it stuck on something while she played and ran around since the tubes hang down on the outside of her body. I was ready for the new port. I have never been good around blood or needles, but I am proud of myself for being strong enough to care for her in all of these ways. It is crazy what you will do for your children as a parent. Nothing else matters when it comes to their health and safety. I was willing to do whatever it took to get Alayna back to normal.

Before she was released, we found out she was carrying 95% of Mikey's DNA. Once a donor's cells take root in your body, you have two separate sets of DNA represented in your tissue. I hadn't realized Alayna would have Mikey's DNA for the rest of her life. Our situation had created a unique bond between the two of them, and I can't wait to see them together when they are older. I am sure Mikey will find a way to hold it over her head a time or two, but who could blame him? He did save her life after all.

Alayna enjoyed being out of her circle room in the hospital. The circle designs on the ceiling created its' name. Looking back, she did amazing the whole time she was stuck in there. She didn't complain about not being able to leave a single time. I am amazed by her. She gave me the strength to get through our situation. If she could do it, so could I. We have come so far, we got through her chemo, we got through her transplant, and we were *finally* leaving the hospital.

At the Ronald McDonald House, we tried to be outside as much as possible. The cool, fall weather was slowly turning into winter, and we wanted to get fresh air for as long as possible. Alayna wasn't required to wear a mask outside, as long as people weren't around. She enjoyed the freedom from the mask, she hated wearing it. Anywhere else, she was required to wear it. You never know who could walk by with an illness.

She was still on a metabolic diet as well so any food that had been opened or cooked had to be thrown away within an hour. Nothing could be saved or reheated because bacteria will begin to grow on the food in that short amount of time, and it could make her sick. Her blood pressure had remained stable thanks to the medication they started her on. She will stay on that medication until she stops taking Cyclosporine.

* * *

Alayna did great during the surgery to get her new port. After a short stay in recovery, we were able to go back home. No-not home. I kept finding myself calling our room in the Ronald McDonald House that, and immediately corrected myself. It wasn't home. But in two months, we will go home. We just had to make it a little while longer. The only aftermath of the surgery was a cut on her chest where they inserted it. Alayna didn't like the look of it, it scared her. It was an odd cut, you can see the port under her skin as there is a bump on her chest.

Before long, Halloween arrived, and Alayna happened to have an appointment with Courtney at the hospital. For the longest time, Alayna has loved cows. They were her favorite animal. Both her and Mikey dressed up as the beloved animal. Courtney was dressed up as Poppy from Trolls. Alayna loves the movie so she loved her costume as well although it did take her a minute to warm up. I, on the other hand, found it difficult to have a serious conversation with a troll.

After the exam, the staff paraded through the hallways, giving candy to all of the children. We finished just in time to watch. Alayna had fun looking at all of the costumes and gathering the candy. She was even featured in a newspaper article about the parade. The photographer took pictures of Alayna and Mikey in their cow costumes, it was adorable.

* November *

When we were preparing for the transplant, the doctors had told us that another side effect caused by the Cyclosporine would be hair growth on the shoulders and back. They weren't lying when they warned it would be crazy. By the middle of November, Alayna's eyebrows became super thick, and her back, arms, and legs were extremely hairy. We joked around, calling her our baby monkey.

I was completely wrong when I thought her new port would be a game-changer. Honestly, Alayna would've done better with an IV. She hates having her port accessed. The area the port is in was extremely sensitive. We put numbing cream on before her clinic visits, but it didn't make much of a difference. We had to hold down her arms, legs, and head while she screams and makes herself hot and sweaty. I hated it, but I became used to it. I found myself slowly becoming desensitized to everything.

I wanted everything to be behind us, I wanted to be home. I tried my hardest to stay positive for everyone, but it was really taking a toll on me. My mom came to one of her clinic appointments and witnessed firsthand what a visit was like. She hadn't been to one before and she was shocked. She had never seen Alayna that worked up before. I couldn't blame her, it was hard to watch.

Alayna's levels have been excellent and she only needed a red blood cell transfusion once since getting released. All of her levels remained steadily rising. Meanwhile, life at the Ronald McDonald House was becoming stressful. Being cooped up in the two small rooms was beginning to get to us. Chris and I began to fight all of the time over silly things. I felt like I was the only one paying attention to the clock for her medication times and keeping track of fluid and food intake.

Chris had started back at his work. I found the origin of our problems was my jealousy that he could get out and socialize. I also began struggling with emotions of hurtfulness. I expected certain family members to check in more than they did. I knew everyone had their own lives. I knew I could check in first. But there was always something going on and I would lose track of time and forget. There was always an excuse from both ends. When I mentioned it to my dad, he told me, "Well, maybe they don't know how or what even to say." It made sense, and I knew they didn't mean any harm by it. But I still hurt, nonetheless. Sometimes it seemed like it was Alayna and me against the world.

The Ronald McDonald House has been amazing and the staff has been super accommodating to make sure we are comfortable. As thankful as we are for the Ronald McDonald House, it wasn't home. Lately when by myself with the kids, even going down to the kitchen was stressful for me. Half of the time, neither of the kids wanted to come, or Alayna couldn't go because there were too many people. I was constantly running up and down, checking on kids and food. I think it would most certainly be easier if Alayna wasn't a transplant patient. Meanwhile, Chris and I were trying to work together and not fight. The kids pick up on our negative energy, and they don't need that.

One day, Alayna told me she missed the green house. That was her name for our home due to its' green color. Moments before, I was browsing through social media. Everyone was sharing how much fall fun they were having, from carving pumpkins to traveling to pumpkin patches. I became bitter looking at picture after picture and ended up logging off. Looking at my daughter, who wanted to go home, and my son, who was dragged into this, I wished our lives were normal. At that moment, I wanted more than anything to scoop both of the kids into my arms and take them to a pumpkin patch so they can pick out their own pumpkins. The more I thought about it, the worse I felt. I would never wish for anyone to be in my situation right now.

Towards the end of the month, we received good news from the doctors. Since Thanksgiving was coming soon, and Alayna's levels were rising with no complications, they said we could venture a little further from the hospital. Chris' Aunt Trish and Uncle Scott live in Macedonia, which was only about twenty-five minutes away. The kids and I were super excited to finally leave. A change of scenery for everyone would be nice.

I was ecstatic at the fact an end was near. But at the same time, I was bummed. Now that I knew there was an end in sight, it would feel like forever until we were finally there. It was so close, but so far away. I feared the days would drag on now. Thanksgiving, however, ended up being really nice. Alayna and Mikey had a blast playing with a Number's family marble game that Scott and Trish have.

* December *

Day in and day out, it was the same routine. Alayna turned four on the 15th. I was sad she couldn't spend it at home, but we were able to throw her a party in the community room.

Her birthday theme was Toy Story 4. She originally wanted Pinocchio, but they don't make those decorations, so Toy Story was her next choice. Both movies have been on her rotation of favorites. We had pizza and cake while we watched Alayna open her presents. I was excited to see my family I hadn't seen in months, I knew Chris and the kids were too.

Alayna and Aunt Trish put together a paper Forky. Aunt Bre had fun putting one together too. Mikey enjoyed playing with the helium balloons. After the crafts, Alayna went running to the tattoos, a favorite thing of hers. With the help of Chris, she gave herself a tattoo. She then picked one out for her cousin Skylar and applied it for her. I spent most of my time helping the kids and talking with family. Aunts, Uncles, cousins, grandparents, and a couple of others who were healthy had all come. Alayna was sad to see everyone go when the time came, but we all had a great time.

A couple of days later, Alayna was ready for Christmas. She began talking about what she was going to ask Santa for Christmas. I sadly realized that I wouldn't be able to take the kids to a local mall to see Santa Claus this year. But, the more I thought about it, I realized where I was. I was at a children's hospital. With a few quick calls, I was about to make arrangements for Santa to come to visit Alayna and Mikey.

The day of Santa's arrival was here, and we found out there was a holiday parade up the street. We made sure to bundle the kids up in coats, hats, and gloves before heading out. Halfway through the parade, we were frozen to the core. The kids enjoyed seeing the floats, but they were cold. Santa, of course, wasn't until the very end. Remembering the walkway between hospitals going above the road, Chris lead us to the hospital.

I wished we would have gone there from the start. There were only a couple of people around, and the view was perfect. The kids could see everything without taller adults blocking their way. Alayna stood from the window with her mask on, watching everything below her intently. And then Santa came into view. Right before he passed beneath us, he locked eyes with Alayna. He stood up from his seat and blew her the biggest kiss. Alayna loved it! She went crazy, exclaiming to everyone that Santa blew her a kiss. It brought tears to my eyes. That gentleman made Alayna feel so special. I wish I could've known who he was so I could personally go and thank him. The kindness he showed to my daughter warmed my heart. I love what the people in this community do for the kids. It is rare to see kindness in our world. These kids, who deserve it more than anyone, are showered in it.

When we got back to our room, Alayna got ready for Santa's visit. After dinner, Santa had arrived. Being the paranoid mother I had become, I double-checked he wasn't sick. Once he confirmed he wasn't, I revealed him to Alayna and Mikey. He personally came into our room, rather than us going to the main hall, so Alayna wouldn't have to wear her mask.

Santa brought little gifts for the kids, two of them being special rocks from the North Pole. He told Alayna to hold them if she ever felt scared. Alayna gave him a toothy smile as he handed her the rock. She loves rocks, she enjoys collecting them. Back at home, she had a whole collection. She then got on Santa's lap and told him she wanted a microphone stand for Christmas so she could sing and play her toy guitar like Ash, the porcupine from the movie Sing. I tried to get a picture with both of the kids on his lap, and Mikey began screaming. It matches last year's picture perfectly.

After I had gotten my fill of pictures, Alayna wanted to take Santa to see the other children staying at the Ronald McDonald House. She put on her mask before grabbing his hand and leading him out of the room. The staff had a chair waiting for him in the dining area, and Alayna brought him right to it. Lately, she had come out of her shell. Before being hospitalized, it would take her a few minutes to warm up to people, even family. Now, she was going right up to strangers carrying on conversations. We said goodbye to Santa, and Alayna made sure to promise him she would leave out cookies and milk for him.

I had started making trips home to unpack our belongings little by little. I paid for a cleaning service to come in and clean the house because the last thing I wanted to do when I finally got home was clean. The day the cleaning service arrived I had went home to let them in and wash sheets. As I was putting clean sheets on Alayna's bed, I couldn't help but feel anxiously excited. I felt like I did when I was pregnant with her as we got her nursery ready and wanting everything perfect. Just staring at the crib knowing it would be filled with a baby in a few days. Only this time, that same baby had now turned into a special four-year-old girl with a twin bed awaiting her arrival. Nick and Bre had also met me at the house to help me put up a Christmas tree. Alayna and Mikey could decorate it when we got home. Before they left, they helped me finish wrapping the kids' gifts. I was ready to come home.

Chapter 9

Home

The day was finally here. We were finally going home. On the morning of Friday, December 20th, we arrived at the clinic for a final visit before Christmas. Laying on the bed in Alayna's room were two stockings overflowing with little goodies. One for Mikey, and one for Alayna. After they opened their stockings, two people came in holding Build-A-Bear boxes. Alayna got a bear dressed in a red dress and a matching headband. Mikey got a stuffed dog, Chase from Paw Patrol.

Of course, the blood work ended up putting a damper on our good spirits, as it usually does. But little to Alayna's knowledge, she had a special surprise waiting for her. The Oncology/Hematology offered to sponsor our family for

Christmas. When a social worker approached me with the idea earlier in the month, I was hesitant. I hated having to ask for help, even though in this case, we weren't asking. But after thinking about it, I decided to accept the offer. After all we have been through, these kids deserved to be spoiled.

As soon as the blood work was finished, the nurses wheeled in a cart overflowing with gifts. Mikey and Alayna were overjoyed opening up all of their Christmas presents. Seeing how happy they were, I knew I had made the right choice. They have been away from home for months, dealing with surgeries and endless medications without complaint. These angels deserved it. I thanked the staff for the gifts. It was such a nice surprise to the kids, and I greatly appreciated it.

Just a short while later, it was finally time to hit the road and go home. 96 days ago, we left our normal lives behind and began our stay at the hospital. The whole way home, I remembered sitting in the same spot, on the same roads, experiencing the complete opposite emotions as I was then. Our normally long drive ended up seeming short. Before long, we were pulling into our driveway.

Watching Alayna's expression was priceless. She was all smiles as she repeated over and over, "It feels so good to be home."

For the first time in months, a calming sense of relief swept through my body. Looking at how happy the kids were, I felt as if a million pounds was lifted from my shoulders. If you would have asked me what future I saw for my family, I wouldn't have been able to answer. We had already been through so much, and there was so much uncertainty regarding the future. But, I had hope. I was so thankful for the outcome of everything.

With tears in my eyes, I looked at Chris and whispered, "We made it." Three months of unpacked luggage and Christmas gifts soon filled my kitchen. Simply looking at the mountainous pile gave me anxiety. Anyone who knows me knows I cannot relax until everything is where it belongs. So, I did just that. About two hours later, everything was unpacked and put away.

A couple of weeks ago, Alayna picked out a Christmas tree and some ornaments online for her bedroom. She was eager to get it up and decorated. Together, we readied her room for Christmas. By the end, she was worn out. Naturally, I ended up decorating the big tree in the living room by myself. We couldn't get a real tree this year because bacteria grow in the water inside of the stand. Alayna still needed to avoid any bacteria and germs. House plants weren't allowed either.

Before I knew it, it was bedtime. Chris and I weren't sure how tonight would go considering we have all slept in the same room for the last three months. Alayna did amazing. She was excited to sleep in her own bed, in her own room. Mikey did okay, but he ended up fussing a little bit. It turned out better than what both Chris and I expected.

The next morning came, and we were slowly falling into a routine. Chris left early to bring the dog's home. It was a happy reunion, filled with lots of kisses and tail wagging. Alayna had become quite taken to Rico, she constantly wanted him by her. A little while later, my mom, Nick, and Bre came down for an early Christmas. We ordered pizza and wings, a delicacy we greatly missed. Alayna had her own pizza we made from home because she still couldn't eat out due to her diet restrictions.

We spent our evening relaxing, talking, and laughing. The kids opened up a couple more gifts from their aunt and uncle. My dad ended up showing up too, with a surprise. He bought the kids a Razor to ride around in the yard. Mikey and Alayna spent the rest of the night pretending to ride the razor in the living room. Bedtime came soon, and Mikey was knocked out from our eventful day. Alayna didn't want to sleep when everyone was over, but she was out within minutes too. I was grateful for how easily they adjusted to being in their own beds.

Christmas Eve is normally spent at my Grandma Rhea's house. However, she was getting over being sick, and we didn't want to take any chances. We stayed home and spent our evening watching Christmas movies. Grammy was staying the night so she could be here in the morning to watch both of them open their presents. I baked cookies, which Alayna put on a plate on the mantle with a cup of milk.

The next morning, we woke up to a tree filled with presents. Santa came! Our second floor has a balcony overlooking the living room. Alayna and Mikey's rooms were on the ends of it. Alayna woke up early and saw all of the presents below. She ran into Mikey's room and woke him up too.

Alayna checked to see if Santa ate his cookies and drank his milk, which he did. There was also a special note laying for her on the counter, sitting beside her digital camera. The note said while he was putting out presents, he noticed her camera. He decided to take a picture of himself by the Christmas tree. Alayna thought the picture was the funniest thing ever and made sure to show everyone. She will cherish that picture forever.

The kids excitedly began to open their presents. Alayna got the microphone stand she wanted so badly. She put on a show of singing and dancing all morning. We had a mess to clean up afterward, but it was worth it. I missed seeing the happy smiles on their faces.

That afternoon, we went to my cousin Heather's house. We weren't able to leave until we received confirmation that everyone there was healthy. Our family was excellent at communicating their health with us, they knew how dangerous it could be for Alayna. A good majority of our big family hadn't seen Alayna since we left all of those months ago. Our arrival brought big hugs to all of us. Alayna loved every minute of it and made sure everyone got to see her picture of Santa.

Before lunch, we all took the hands of each other in a giant circle around the kitchen. Rick, Heather's husband, began to say grace. He prayed for all of the sick families. He talked about how grateful we were for Alayna's quick recovery and that she could be here to spend Christmas with the family. By the end of it, I was bawling. It was truly a blessing she was able to be home and spend this special day with family.

After a long, joyful day spent with loved ones, it was finally time to go home. The trunk of our car was filled with even more gifts. These kids are spoiled. At home, we hooked Alayna up to fluids through her NG tube. She didn't drink enough while we were at Heather's. She still needs to drink plenty of fluids because of her medication. She was beginning to wean off of Cyclosporine as well, though it would still be several weeks until she would be completely off of it.

Thankfully, Alayna hadn't experienced any signs of Graft-versus-host Disease. Our original plan was for her to be on Cyclosporine for at least a year. But she is exceeding and progressing so well it's no longer needed. Regardless, there will always be a chance of her developing Graft-versus-host, but the chances are very slim. Almost as slim as catching a one-in-a-million disease, like Aplastic Anemia. Or winning the lottery. But of course, we won the disease, not the lottery. I am glad I am finally able to have a sense of humor about everything. Alayna has done amazing, and it was a weight lifted off of my shoulders. I quickly learned you can't be sad forever. You need to live your life, and Alayna's was just getting started.

My New Year's resolution for myself was to not dwell on the past. I am not going to stress about the future or the unknown. Alayna had continued to do amazing. We took it one day at a time, celebrating every victory, no matter how small. It was crazy getting her labs back and not seeing an 'L' for low beside everything.

Our world was turned upside down in such a short amount of time. All of the genetic tests have come back negative prior to the transplant so Aplastic Anemia is not hereditary. With Alayna's Aplastic Anemia diagnosis being idiopathic, it's not very settling, and sometimes I found myself wracking my brain for possibilities. Thinking like that could drive somebody crazy. I told myself to stop, take a deep breath, and focus on my resolution.

I will forever be thankful for Alayna's fast recovery. Everything went so quickly as opposed to everything getting dragged out if she developed any issues. I also decided to focus more on my self-care. I am the main caretaker of the kids and the house. It became hard to go to weekly doctor appointments, remember to count fluids, and dispense all medications, all the while managing the household. I quickly got stressed, and the kids would feel it. I was always putting others' feelings first and before mine. But not anymore. I will continue to help and care for others, but I won't let it drag me down anymore.

I made a promise to myself and Alayna that I would be her biggest advocate. I want to educate others on the rare disease known as Aplastic Anemia. I want to show people the importance of bone marrow transplants and being on a registry list. Donating blood and bone marrow is lifesaving. God only knows where we would be without Mikey's bone marrow, and all of the blood Alayna was able to receive.

I always knew how important donating blood was, but it was never at the top of my priority list. Until you live a life where getting blood becomes a life or death matter, you never realize just how important it is. I want to open people's eyes and make them realize by donating just a few pints of blood, they can save countless lives. Lives of those who could die without it. I am thankful for how advanced the study of medicine has become. Without it, Alayna wouldn't have survived.

* January *

January 2, 2020. Day +100. We finally made it to our goal. Today, Alayna was supposed to be discharged from the Ronald McDonald House and come home. We are so thankful she was able to come home early. As of today, her metabolic diet was officially over. We still had to be careful, but she could finally eat from a drive-through or restaurant menu.

For weeks, Alayna had been wanting a cheese roll-up from Taco Bell and french fries from Wendy's. We weren't 100% sold on Taco Bell yet, so we went to Wendy's and got her some fries. We only asked that they were made fresh, we didn't mind waiting in the car. Alayna was so happy when she finally got them. Her giant, toothy smile made me realize we did it. We made it 100 days without any problems. Wendy's french fries became a special treat after her weekly doctor appointments. She deserved them.

Chapter 10

Hope

A couple of weeks ago, I went out with my step-sister, Amanda. At the restaurant, I began talking with the bartender and found we both had daughters named Alayna. She started telling me stories of herself and her daughter, before abruptly stopping. She apologized, assuming she was boring me. Smiling, I told her I was stuck at home every day with the kids. It was nice to talk with another adult. I then proceeded to tell her about my Alayna, and everything she has been through.

The bartender was taken aback, tears in her eyes. I will never forget what she said next. "I never would have guessed what you have been through. You seem to have yourself so put together."

I thanked her, reassuring her that I don't feel put together. I still struggle daily. Every day, my anxiety is on overload. As she walked away, I thought to myself, yet another lesson Alayna has taught me. Never judge a book by its cover. My encounter shows why you shouldn't judge someone by how they look and be kind to *everyone*. You never know what is going on in their life. Just because they look like they have their life put together doesn't mean they do. Someone could look unbelievably happy, but go home and fall apart.

I don't want people to look at our family or Alayna any differently. I don't want them to pity us. I want them to look at our family and see a brave, little girl brimming with life. I want them to see a strong, little boy who is prepared to take on anything. I don't want what we went through to label any of us. I want our label to be the fact that we got through it, together.

As I sit in bed while everyone else is asleep, my mind continues to wander. A few months prior to our wedding, in May, Amanda lost her husband. Three children lost their father. We lost a beloved family member. Not only was it unexpected, but it was also tragic. At the funeral, I remember the pastor saying something along the lines of, "Think of your life as an unfinished quilt. When you look down at this quilt, it doesn't make sense yet because it's not finished. But as you move on in life, and piece your quilt together more, it will eventually all make perfect sense."

Maybe Alayna was supposed to get sick. Maybe God knew Alayna was strong enough to handle it. Maybe this is my calling to become her biggest advocate and share her story. Maybe all of this happened for a reason. I learned priceless life-lessons that I wouldn't have learned otherwise. It brought the four of us closer as a family. The one thing I do know for sure is that I need to share our story. I need to bring light to my daughter's rare disease and everything I learned because of it.

On Day +143, Alayna officially stopped taking her Cyclosporine and had her NG tube taken out. It is those tiny milestones that we can celebrate because it shows how far we have come. She will continue to be closely monitored until September. After, she will go in yearly until the age of twenty-five for a check-up. The hospital's multidisciplinary survivorship clinic will monitor her for late effects that can be caused by chemotherapy.

I love sharing Alayna's story with people, especially those who are facing the same predicament that we were once in. I want to give them hope that their situation can get better. I want to give them the courage and strength they'll need to carry on. I want them to know it is okay to be mad or upset.

But it is not okay to stay that way. Staying in good spirits is important because your mood will rub off on everyone.

I need to practice what I preach. I recently have found myself, once again, struggling emotionally. Just when it felt like I could finally breathe a little more, a couple of days ago, I got the news that my cousin Angela got into a tragic accident and put on life support. She was 37. I didn't know how to accept the news. In February, only a few months ago, she came to visit. Alayna was on a slinky kick at the time, and Angie, as we called her, brought her one. We talked about visiting her and her family in Georgia this summer once Alayna was restriction-free and Alayna could collect some sea shells from the beach there.

Angie had a wonderful husband and four amazing boys. She had come such a long way from the person she was when younger. I have no clue how she managed it, considering she raised four boys. I have always admired her, she was such a free spirit. Angie was also one of Chris's best friends as they grew up together. He was having a hard time accepting the whole situation as well.

At the same time, the Coronavirus pandemic was beginning to spread across the country. A social distancing order was put into place for all of the United States. We have already spent months in quarantine, and now we are being told we will have to spend months more. We can't take any chances of Alayna catching it, meaning we have to be extremely cautious. This summer was supposed to be spent having fun without any restrictions on Alayna's end.

We were given one last chance to say goodbye to Angie before she was taken off of life support. Chris and I both wanted to leave the second we heard. But, as much as it broke our hearts, we couldn't. It put us at risk for catching the virus, and we couldn't bring it home to Alayna. Not being able to tell her goodbye was eating away at me. Fortunately, my dad and brother were able to go. They took my grandma with them as well.

Luckily, Angie's best friend was able to call me and she put the phone up to Angie's ear. I was able to talk to her one last time and tell her goodbye and how much we loved her. It was hard, but it gave me the closure that I needed. I will forever be grateful for our final moment together. We are only given one life, and we need to make the best of it. Enjoy every moment life has to offer because you never know when things could drastically change.

* * *

In late March, Alayna officially stopped taking all of her medications. However, we did start her back on an appetite stimulant again. She has always been a picky eater. It is common for kids to lose their appetites after undergoing a bone marrow transplant. I fear her problem is she hasn't been burning enough energy to feel hungry. We made an effort to spend our days playing outside and going on long walks. She gets tired easily, but we will get her back to normal soon. I have faith.

As far as her follow up appointments, she goes to the clinic every month. Due to the pandemic, her port removal surgery has been put on hold. To her dismay, she still has to get her port flushed monthly to prevent it from getting clogged. Our governor has planned on giving elective surgeries the green light in early May. We are hoping to be able to schedule the removal surgery soon.

At a recent clinic visit, Alayna was able to start receiving a few vaccinations. She was not happy about it, but I was. Not only did it give her more protection, but it also meant that her body was strong enough for the shots. It was a little nerve wracking but neither her nor Mikey ever reacted bad to a vaccination, luckily. The doctors didn't expect any issues.

Mikey has handled this whole process like a champ. I am so proud of this little boy. Who knew such a young, little boy could be such a big miracle? His whole world was flipped upside down. I struggled emotionally for him, as well as myself. He was my baby, and I was missing out on doing fun things with him. My focus was barely put on him. I couldn't take him to places like Disney on Ice or Sky Zone to have fun. But I knew it was for the best, and once Alayna is healthy enough, we will go out and do everything we can. These kids deserve it.

Aplastic anemia is considered a critical illness, meaning Alayna gets a wish from the Make-A-Wish Foundation. She has dreamed for the longest time of going to Disney World. When I asked her what she wanted as a wish, her immediate response was to go to Disney World and meet her favorite character, Woody, from Toy Story. The Make-A-Wish team was supposed to come and grant her wish this spring, but yet again, the Coronavirus has put another event on back hold for the time being.

Way back in September of 2019, we planned a honeymoon in Florida. That was when everything with Alayna was getting started, and we ended up having to cancel it. It wouldn't have been safe for her. We have hope to make it up in the summer and go on a mini honeymoon. But who knows, considering we are currently stuck inside because of a pandemic. We are already pros at social-distancing, what's a couple of months more?

We did end up having a setback, but it didn't have to do with Alayna. Chris was laid off of work. They shut the doors. They offered him money to move us down by Columbus, where they were relocating. But we couldn't do that, especially because Alayna's care is up here. Luckily, he had a feeling something like this was going to happen. He was already in the process of starting his own business.

At this point, my only worry is health insurance. Recently, I was browsing and saw an article that priced it for a family of four. The monthly amount was ridiculous.

There was no way we would be able to meet it each month. But I know we will figure it out, and everything will be fine. We just have to take it one day at a time.

I can't help but say once again how grateful Chris and I are for our family, friends, and community. We felt like we had hit rock bottom. The odds were against us, and it is a common saying that having a sick child can tear a family apart. It's not easy, but we are doing it. There were hurtful words passed between us along the way. We both questioned each other over and over about what we wanted out of life. But here we are, still together and pushing through the storm. We are stronger than our tragedy.

As our storm passes, I can see the blue skies behind the clouds. There will always be tough times, but making those tough times better is what matters the most. The outlook you have on a situation can change your entire viewpoint. When you're having a bad day, remember it could be so much worse. If I am having a bad day from exhaustion, mixed with the stir-crazy feeling from being trapped at home, I remind myself how lucky I am. Alayna's recovery was flawless, and we are at home, rather being inside the hospital or the Ronald McDonald House.

Unfortunately, some families aren't as lucky as we are. Even though some children lose their fight, it doesn't mean they aren't strong. It means they are the strongest out of us all. It means they fought battles unimaginable to us, and they are finally getting the peace they deserve. I sympathize with parents bringing in hospice. While it doesn't seem fair, we have to have faith and remind ourselves that this is all a part of God's mighty plan.

I always remind myself to celebrate every victory, no matter how small. Every step forward, even a tiny stumble, is worth the elated cheers. It is important to remember that you are not alone. Someone is always there, you just have to let them in. Never assume you can handle it all on your own because you can't. You need the support of anyone who offers, a lesson I struggled to learn. It took me a while to realize it, but we had an army of people behind our backs, cheering us on.

Last, but not least, we are all on this journey together. I have faith you will get through whatever storm clouds your way. No matter how bad it gets, have hope. Hope can break through any darkness, it is a bright light amongst the seemingly endless black. It is amazing how strong you can be when you think you don't have any strength left to give.

Thank you for listening to our story. I will forever remain Alayna's biggest advocate, sharing her story to all who will listen. I hope we shed light on the importance of keeping hope in the darkest of storms. We wouldn't have been able to get through it without it. We will forever be grateful for the support from our family, friends, community, and the wonderful medical team of Akron Children's Hospital. We wouldn't have made it without you. Thank you.

Acknowledgements

First and foremost, I would like to thank my cousin, Skylar Blumenauer, for editing and proofreading. Skylar dedicated months of her time to help me make this story possible while still attending school. When I realized I wanted to make my journal for Alayna into a story to give others hope, I knew she would be great at helping as she loves reading and writing. Skylar had previously won two first place awards locally for writing in the Patriots Pen and Voice of Democracy writing contests. She helped organize all of my wording and made my emotions into words while making everything flow so well together. As well as, all of the offered great suggestions and ideas where more details would be beneficial. Thanks Sky, I couldn't have done this without you!

Secondly, I want to thank my cousin, Heather Geis-Heather. When Alayna was first admitted to the hospital, Heather did a great job at keeping the whole family up to date on the details so we didn't have to constantly reach out to each individual, and all of our focus could be on Alayna. Heather is also the owner of her graphic design business, Geis Graphics. She is an amazing graphic designer as well as event planner. She helped come up with all of the designs for the AlaynaStrong Benefit. Heather was able to gather all of the family and come up with ideas for the benefit, everyone did an amazing job. I don't think I could ever repay you as I know your blood, sweat and tears went into everything you did and we love you so very much for all you have done. You were there when I needed to vent, and you never judged, you always listened.

I also want to thank all of my immediate family. My brother and sister-in-law, Nick and Bre Margazano, my grandma, Rhea Hayes, my mom, Barb Gore and my dad and step mother, Joe and Michelle Margazano. You guys stepped up immediately when everything went crazy and helped watch Mikey under last minute circumstances and were always there to lend a hand when needed. Of course, as well as helping with all you did of the benefit. I love you all, thank you!

I want to thank my husband, Chris Numbers. I couldn't imagine being on this crazy roller coaster of life with anyone else. I know I can be a lot to handle most of the time so thank you for keeping me grounded and being my rock when I need it. Life hasn't been easy along the way, but we are making lemonade with our lemons when given the chance. I love you.

Of course, our circumstances would be very different without our little superhero, our son, Michael J. Numbers. I remember how shocked we were when we found out we were expecting you. I didn't think I would be able to love another child as much, boy was I wrong. You have brought so much joy into our lives. You were the missing piece of our puzzle as you complete our family so much. I remember buying a sign for your nursery when I was pregnant, "Little Boys Are Just Superheroes in Disguise". Was that a sign that you were going to do something so great? You have definitely completed your mission that God sent you here to do. I can't wait to watch you grow and see what else your future holds. I love you forever and ever, my bubby.

Last but not least, Alayna wouldn't be where she is today without the wonderful help, care and support of everyone along the way and in between:

Dr. Steven Kuerbitz, MD
Courtney Culbertson, MSN, APRN-CPNP, CPHON
Dr. John Fargo, DO

Dr. Nicholas Farris, MD

Dr. Marla Kantaras, MD

All staff and nurses of The Showers Family Center for Childhood Cancer and Blood Disorders/Unit 5600

Heather Lanfranchi, LISW-S

Ronald McDonald House-Akron, Ohio

Scott and Trish Numbers

Michelle Numbers and Jonathan Gregg

Minerva Herrera

Courtney Black

Maelynn Black

Michael and Connie Numbers

Author House Publishing

MMR Photography-Katelynn Ross

AAMDS Foundation

Aplastic Anemia Awareness Group

Printed in the United States
By Bookmasters